WOMEN
AND SPORTS

BY A.W. BUCKEY

ReferencePoint
Press®

San Diego, CA

© 2019 ReferencePoint Press, Inc.
Printed in the United States

For more information, contact:
ReferencePoint Press, Inc.
PO Box 27779
San Diego, CA 92198
www.ReferencePointPress.com

LIBRARY OF CONGRESS CATALOGING-IN-PUBLICATION DATA

Names: Buckey, A. W., author.
Title: Women and sports / by A.W. Buckey.
Description: San Diego, California : ReferencePoint Press, Inc., [2019] |
   Series: Women and society | Audience: Grades: 9 to 12. | Includes
   bibliographical references and index.
Identifiers: LCCN 2018038250 (print) | LCCN 2018041645 (ebook) | ISBN
   9781682825501 (ebook) | ISBN 9781682825495 (hardback)
Subjects: LCSH: Sports for women--History. | Sports for women--Social
   aspects. | Sports for women--Management. | Women athletes--Social
   conditions.
Classification: LCC GV709 (ebook) | LCC GV709.B83 2019 (print) | DDC
   796.082--dc23
LC record available at https://lccn.loc.gov/2018038250

CONTENTS

IMPORTANT EVENTS IN WOMEN'S HISTORY   4

INTRODUCTION   6
The Horizon Problem

CHAPTER 1   10
What Is the History Behind Women and Sports?

CHAPTER 2   22
What Is the Culture Around Women and Sports?

CHAPTER 3   42
What Is the Business Side of Women and Sports?

CHAPTER 4   56
What Is the Future of Women and Sports?

Source Notes   70
For Further Research   74
Index   76
Image Credits   79
About the Author   80

IMPORTANT EVENTS IN
WOMEN'S HISTORY

1960
Wilma Rudolph becomes the first American woman to win three Olympic gold medals in track and field.

1928
After years of controversy, the Olympic Games allow women to compete in five track and field events.

1892
Coach Senda Berenson Abbott introduces women's basketball at Smith College in Massachusetts.

1952
For the first time, women and men compete together in open equestrian events in the Olympics.

1880	1900	1920	1940	1960

1926
Gertrude Ederle becomes the first woman to swim the English Channel, setting a world record in the process.

1966
Bobbi Gibb becomes the first woman to run the Boston Marathon.

1943
The All-American Girls Softball League, later called the All-American Girls Professional Baseball League, is established.

1972
Title IX passes, requiring schools and universities to provide men and women with equal opportunities to play sports.

1978
The Amateur Sports Act of 1978 bans discrimination in amateur sports and encourages sports opportunities for people with disabilities.

1996
The Women's National Basketball Association (WNBA) is approved by the National Basketball Association (NBA) Board of Governors.

2017
Tennis player Serena Williams wins her twenty-third Grand Slam title, collecting the most singles titles of any tennis player in the modern era.

1970   1980   1990   2000   2010

1981
Tennis players Billie Jean King and Martina Navratilova come out as gay.

1999
Heather Nabozny becomes the first female head groundskeeper in the history of Major League Baseball.

2012
Women's boxing is included in the 2012 Summer Olympics. For the first time, women participate in every sport at the Olympic Games.

2006
Pat Summitt becomes the first women's college basketball coach to earn more than $1 million in a season.

1973
Billie Jean King defeats Bobby Riggs in the famous "Battle of the Sexes" tennis match.

THE HORIZON
PROBLEM

Ashima Shiraishi looked up at a problem. She was at a large rock
near Mount Hiei in Japan. Shiraishi is a rock climber who specializes
in bouldering, or climbing short rock routes with no ropes or nets.
Bouldering routes are known as problems, and they are rated by difficulty.
This problem, Horizon, was rated V15. That made it one of the most
difficult problems in the world. In order to reach the top, Shiraishi would
have to use her strength to push upward, holding on to tiny cracks in
the rock.

She had fallen off the boulder several times in the past. But on
March 22, 2016, her coach wrote, she looked "fierce, focused, and
strong."[1] When Shiraishi completed Horizon, she became the first female
climber in the world to conquer a V15. But that wasn't all. She was also
the youngest person of any gender to complete a problem of that level. At
the time of the climb, she was fourteen years old and a straight-A student
in ninth grade. She finished the route on her spring break.

At fourteen, Shiraishi was already used to breaking records. She started climbing at age six on a boulder in Central Park in New York City, her hometown. Shiraishi remembers being amazed by the climbers she saw there: "There seemed to be a method to their movements," she recalled, "almost like they were slowly dancing to the top of the rock."[2] She decided to try it too and found she was a natural. Shiraishi still thinks of rock climbing this way. When she studies a problem, trying to figure out which route to take, she sways her arms like a dancer in motion.

By age eight, Shiraishi had won her first Bouldering National Championship. At ten, she became the youngest person to climb a V13. She won Youth World Championships for two different types of climbing three years in a row. Shiraishi breaks records for climbers of any gender, but male and female climbers are ranked separately. According to the International Federation of Sport Climbing, Shiraishi was the eighth-best female climber in the world at the end of 2017.

> "There seemed to be a method to [the climbers'] movements, almost like they were slowly dancing to the top of the rock."[2]
>
> – Ashima Shiraishi, champion rock climber

Shiraishi doesn't like when people say her accomplishments are amazing because she is a girl. "If I was a guy, it would still be really cool, but [people think], 'She's a girl, so that's what makes it better,' or something. I wish people wouldn't think of it that way," she said.[3] Shiraishi doesn't fit some people's ideas of what a star athlete looks like. She is five-foot-one (155 cm) and has a small frame. But she knows that she is strong. She explained, "I never really questioned whether I was weaker than the guys. . . . [Climbing is] a sport that doesn't require you to have a specific body type."[4] She is known throughout the world for her strength, her flexibility, and her ability to approach problems in new and creative ways.

Ashima Shiraishi specializes in bouldering, which is rock climbing short routes with no ropes or nets. She is ranked among the best female rock climbers in the world and hopes to compete in the 2020 Olympics.

In 2020, rock climbing will be added as an Olympic sport for the first time. Shiraishi is training and hopes to represent the United States. Shiraishi is starting to support her professional career through advertising deals with companies. Most sports sponsorship deals go to male athletes, but Shiraishi's star status has attracted sponsors. She has deals with Coca Cola and the outdoor brands The North Face and Petzl. Rock climbing is not well-known as a competitive sport yet, but Shiraishi is excited for its future. "I feel like climbing is just going to keep on getting bigger," she said. "In every country, everywhere, you're surrounded by rocks. There are rocks everywhere in the world."[5]

"I never really questioned whether I was weaker than the guys."[4]
– Ashima Shiraishi, champion rock climber

Sports bring joy and challenge to the lives of many women and girls like Shiraishi. Across the world, women are innovating and pushing boundaries in the world of athletics. But even record-breaking athletes like Shiraishi have to deal with obstacles. A long pattern of gender discrimination in sports can make it more difficult for women to thrive and compete. Female athletes often face stereotypes about how women should behave. They face people who doubt the capabilities of their minds and bodies. They can feel intense pressure to achieve in many areas of life. Women often find that it can be difficult to get the same professional and financial opportunities that men have in sports.

CHAPTER ONE
WHAT IS THE HISTORY BEHIND WOMEN AND SPORTS?

Sports are everywhere in modern life. Most American children play sports growing up, and about 60 percent of American adults describe themselves as sports fans. Successful athletes become stars in media and entertainment. Ancient writings and art show that the history of sports stretches back thousands of years in cultures all around the world. Many early sports evolved from activities that people did in order to survive. For example, the sport of archery evolved from hunting with bows and arrows. Other sports may have started as religious rituals. This includes the Mesoamerican ball game, the first game ever played with a rubber ball. Other sports, such as racing and wrestling, likely developed from fighting and play. And for as long as sports have existed, women have been playing them.

EARLY HISTORY OF WOMEN IN SPORTS

According to historical record, the first Olympic Games were held in Olympia, Greece, in the year 776 BCE. The games were open to competitors from every area of the Greek empire. They began as a

WOMEN ATHLETES IN MYTHOLOGY

Many ancient cultures feature athletic goddesses and heroines in their myths. In Northern Europe, Skadi was the ancient Norse goddess of skiing and hunting. She is famous in ancient Norse stories for loving the mountains. In ancient Norse art, she is pictured on skis. In ancient Greek religion, Artemis was the goddess of hunting. She became known as Diana in Roman mythology.

Greek mythology's most famous woman athlete was named Atalanta. She was a legendary hunter and racer who claimed that she would marry any man who could outrun her. Many men tried and failed to match her speed, and they were killed as a result. Finally, one man was able to win a race against Atalanta only after he distracted her with golden apples.

Another legendary woman athlete, the Mongolian princess Khutulun, may have been based on a real person. According to myths, she was a great-granddaughter of the emperor Genghis Khan and lived in the 1200s. She was an expert in the traditional Mongolian sports of horse riding, archery, and wrestling, becoming famous as an undefeated female wrestler. Like Atalanta, Khutulun refused to marry any man who could not defeat her. She wrestled many men. Since no man could beat her, she finally decided to marry a man of her own choice, without making him lose a wrestling battle first.

religious festival to honor the god Zeus. The first Olympic competition was a footrace, and later Olympic games included fighting and throwing events. No women were allowed as Olympic competitors. But in one corner of the Greek Empire, Sparta, women had their own competitions in which they raced and wrestled each other. Later in Greek history, a festival to honor the goddess Hera included a footrace between women competitors. The story of women in the ancient Olympics has many parallels throughout the history of women's sports. Women have always played sports, but their competitions have often been limited and overshadowed by men's events.

Wrestling, for example, is a very old sport. Although wrestling is often associated with men, there are records of male and female wrestlers throughout the ancient world. In several African societies, women wrestled each other for entertainment and as part of traditional rituals. Ancient Greek women wrestled each other, and this tradition probably continued throughout the Roman Empire as well. In ancient Turkey and Central

Asia, women were valued not just as wrestlers but as archers and horse riders, too.

In many societies, sports participation became divided not just by gender but also by social class. In ancient and medieval China, some upper-class women participated in sports reserved for the elite, such as archery and polo. Meanwhile, in Europe, upper-class medieval women also took part in archery and hunting, while peasant- and middle-class women ran races and played games in their villages. One medieval manuscript shows a group of monks and nuns playing ball games together. In fourteenth-century Hawaii, upper- and working-class people practiced different types of wrestling and martial arts. Working-class Hawaiian men and women boxed and wrestled in official competitions. Ancient Mesoamerican cultures such as the Mayans had a tradition of playing ball games for thousands of years. While most records of the Mesoamerican ball game show male players, there is some evidence that women played the game as well. In North America, many Native American cultures encouraged sports participation among both men and women.

In the 1600s and 1700s, many European cultures discouraged the idea of women's participation in sports. Men argued that physical activity was unladylike for women, especially middle- or upper-class women. Early European settlers in the United States disapproved of women's participation in sports. Sports historian Allen Guttman wrote, "None of the contests that we commonly classify as sports was thought suitable for women. Their sports were limited to husking bees, quilting contests, and other competitions directly related to women's domestic labor."[6] Women were expected to work hard in the home, but not to channel that physical ability into sports.

"[Women's] sports were limited to husking bees, quilting contests, and other competitions directly related to women's domestic labor."[6]
– Allen Guttmann, sports historian

In the 1800s and early 1900s, American society had conflicting ideas about whether women should participate in sports. Many people still did not believe that women were strong enough to handle both physical and mental activity. Some scientists and doctors went so far as to say that exercise was unhealthy and unnatural for women. One doctor working in 1912 wrote an article reflecting popular attitudes at that time about women in sports. He acknowledged that sports had the power to improve women's physical fitness and mental discipline. But the doctor saw this as a potentially dangerous thing, warning that "all forms of athletic sports and most physical exercises tend to make women's figures more masculine."[7] He recommended that all men's sports be made shorter and easier for women to avoid overtiring them. Otherwise, the thinking went, women might faint or suffer heart failure.

Despite these attitudes, some women still became successful athletes. In the 1700s, when boxing matches were popular in England, a woman named Elizabeth Stokes became a well-known prizefighter. She bragged about her talent in the ring. Stokes publicized her skills with newspaper advertisements calling herself the "Invincible City Championess" and challenging other women to bouts.[8] In the 1800s, speed walking contests were popular in America and Europe. One champion of the sport, Bertha von Hillern, was praised by newspapers as "an apostle of muscular religion."[9]

Many of today's most popular sports were developed in the mid-1800s to early 1900s. Baseball, known as America's pastime, came from stick and ball games played by British children. Basketball was invented in Massachusetts in the 1890s. In 1869, Americans played the first intercollegiate football game. And a 1901 handbook called *The Book of Sport* shows proof that golf and tennis were already popular in the United States at that time. With the possible exception of football, all of these sports had significant numbers of female players. Basketball was introduced to players at women's colleges almost immediately after it was invented. However, even early on, women's sports were subject to sexism and stereotypes. For example, basketball coach Senda Berenson wrote in 1903 that the sport could be a good influence on women but that she modified some rules to keep her players from doing "sad unwomanly things."[10] Another example is the first traveling women's baseball team, which was created in the 1800s. Although other women's baseball teams existed during the same era, the players on this traveling team were accused of being prostitutes rather than athletes, so the team didn't last for long.

SPORTS IN THE EARLY TWENTIETH CENTURY

In the early twentieth century many sports were most accessible to members of the upper class. Athletes could play team sports such as football and basketball at elite colleges, and squash and tennis were available at upper-class country clubs. At the turn of the century, many communities tried to make sports available to working-class children. In major cities such as New York and Chicago, urban planners created public parks, tracks, and tennis courts where children could play sports. While these parks were open to girls, they tended to be heavily segregated by race. Many parks and playgrounds were either difficult or impossible for black children to access. In the 1920s and 1930s, children's Little League baseball games became popular among middle-class families. However, Little League baseball remained closed to girls until 1974.

The Olympic Games were revived in 1896, and over the years this developed into the Olympics of today. Women began participating in the Olympics in 1900, but they were allowed to compete in only a few events: tennis, sailing, croquet, equestrian sports, and golf. Many International Olympic Committee (IOC) members were strongly opposed to women's

WOMEN AND BICYCLES

The bicycle was invented in the early 1800s. In the late 1800s, an early form of the modern bicycle, with a steel frame and rubber tires, started to become popular in the United States and Western Europe. During that time, women's rights activists saw the bicycle as a way for women to gain more freedom and self-determination. In the nineteenth century, women faced many social restrictions that limited their ability to walk or travel alone. The bicycle helped change those social rules. One famous slogan said that "woman is riding to suffrage," or the right to vote, "on the bicycle." Bicycles helped introduce new fashions such as bloomers, which looked like puffy cotton pants. Bloomers were much safer for riding than the heavy skirts that were fashionable at the time. Some men reacted poorly to the idea of women on bicycles. They claimed that the freedom to ride made women immoral and irresponsible. For many women, however, learning to ride bicycles offered them a new freedom. In 1895, Frances Willard wrote an essay about her experience learning to ride a bicycle in her fifties. "I wanted to help women to a wider world," she wrote, "for I hold that the more interests women and men can have in common . . . the happier it will be for the home."

Quoted in Jean O'Reilly and Susan K. Cahn, Women and Sports in the United States: A Documentary Reader. Boston, Massachusetts: Northeastern University Press, 2007, p. 16.

participation. Progress in integrating the games was slow, and by 1960, women still made up only 20 percent of Olympics participants.

Nevertheless, international sports competitions such as the Olympics allowed some women to become sports celebrities. Mildred "Babe" Didrikson Zaharias, a legendary athlete from Texas, became famous at the 1932 Olympics for winning three medals in three separate track and field events. Zaharias was an untrained athlete who had only started competing two years before the Olympics. Zaharias later became a champion golfer and basketball player as well. Zaharias was named "the greatest female athlete of the first half of the twentieth century" by *Sports Illustrated* magazine.[11] However, the media sometimes mocked her appearance and straightforward personality, which were perceived by some as too masculine. One of her nicknames in the press was "muscle moll."[12]

Mildred "Babe" Didrikson Zaharias was considered a trailblazer for women in sports, as she won three Olympic medals for track and field in 1932. However, like many female athletes, she was often criticized by media and the public.

In the 1930s and 1940s, women athletes who seemed sexy and feminine were favored by the public and the press. Norwegian ice skater Sonja Henie, who won every skating world championship between 1927 and 1937, became a global celebrity and movie star. Henie, who was famous for her glamorous outfits and dancelike skating style, represented a cute and feminine model of a popular athlete. She earned millions of dollars through endorsements and movie deals and increased the global popularity of figure skating.

When men were drafted to fight in World War II (1939–1945), the United States faced a shortage of male baseball players. This led to the creation of the All-American Girls Professional Baseball League. This professional women's baseball league lasted from 1943 until 1954. Players in the league were required to look feminine, wearing skirts and lipstick at all times. But they were also taken seriously as professional athletes. At its peak, in the 1948 season, the league attracted 910,000 fans to its games. Pitcher Jean Faut remembered her time in the league as a highlight of her life. "The eight seasons I played in the All-American Baseball League were the most exciting, most memorable years of my life," Faut recalled. "The league was extremely competitive, and more so as the years went by. The tougher it got, the more I liked it."[13]

> "The league was extremely competitive, and more so as the years went by. The tougher it got, the more I liked it."[13]
> — *Jean Faut, former professional baseball player*

WOMEN'S SPORTS AND CIVIL RIGHTS

In the 1950s and 1960s, the American civil rights movement worked to dismantle legal racial discrimination and segregation. By the end of the 1950s, all major American sports were officially integrated. Black women athletes such as runner Wilma Rudolph and tennis player Althea Gibson made history with their accomplishments. Rudolph astounded fans at the 1960 Rome Olympics when she broke three world records in the 100-meter, 200-meter, and 4x100-relay events. In 1957, Gibson won a Wimbledon title and US Championship, becoming the highest-ranked female tennis player in the world. Although she struggled with racism throughout her career, Gibson served as an inspiration for other black tennis players. Tennis champion Venus Williams, a black woman, once said that she was able to be so successful in tennis "because of people like Althea."[14]

TITLE IX

In the 1960s and 1970s, the fight for women's rights gained popularity and power with a new feminist movement. Prominent feminists of this time worked to boost women's participation in every aspect of public life, fighting against barriers such as wage discrimination and lack of job-training opportunities. The US feminist movement also helped create legislation to boost women's equality in sports. In 1972, Congress passed a series of laws called Title IX. Among other things, the legislation requires that all schools and universities that receive public funding give men and women equal opportunities to play sports. This does not mean that men and women have to play the same sports or that money has to be divided exactly equally between men's and women's programs. Instead, the law states that women need an equal opportunity to play the sports they want to play and equal access to resources such as equipment and practice fields. Title IX dramatically increased women's participation in high school and college sports. Between 1971 and 2001, girls' participation in high school varsity sports increased more than 845 percent, from less than 300,000 athletes to almost 2.8 million. Women's participation in college athletics jumped more than 400 percent.

Title IX was controversial from the beginning of its existence. Opponents of the law claimed that it took away opportunities from male athletes. These critics argued that since men were naturally more interested in sports than women were, the law punished a majority of boys at the expense of a minority of girls. "In the end," one men's wrestling coach argued, "100 percent of the girls are fully accommodated but only 10 percent of the boys are taken care of."[15]

Despite the strides made by women, female athletes have continued to struggle to be taken seriously. In 1973, fifty-five-year-old retired tennis player Bobby Riggs claimed that he could beat any woman in a tennis match. Billie Jean King was a twenty-nine-year-old professional tennis player at the height of her career. She decided to take up Riggs on his challenge. The match between them became known as "The Battle of the Sexes." More than 30,000 people showed up to watch the match. King won three sets in a row to beat Riggs in less than two hours, a symbolic

Tennis player Billie Jean King defended all female athletes in 1973 when she defeated Bobby Riggs in a tennis match known as "The Battle of the Sexes." King challenged Riggs after he claimed he could beat any woman in tennis.

victory for women athletes. "Billie Jean is too good," Riggs said after the match. "Too good. Too quick. She deserved to win it."[16]

The 1960s and 1970s also saw the growth of sports opportunities for men and women with disabilities. The International Sports Organization for the Disabled was founded in 1963, and the first Special Olympics were held five years later. In 1978, Congress passed the Amateur Sports Act of 1978. The law was

> "Billie Jean is too good. Too good. Too quick. She deserved to win it."[16]
> – *Bobby Riggs, tennis player*

aimed at ensuring equality in amateur sports between men and women. It also requires the US Olympic Committee to promote amateur sports opportunities for people with disabilities. The first international Paralympic Games for athletes with physical disabilities was in 1960, with 400 athletes from twenty-three countries competing. In 1968, the first international Special Olympic Games were held for male and female athletes with intellectual disabilities.

GROWTH OF WOMEN'S PROFESSIONAL SPORTS

In the 1990s, a generation of women born after Title IX came of age. It was a powerful era for women's sports in the United States. In 1996, the first professional women's basketball league, the Women's National Basketball Association (WNBA), was founded. American women gained international fame in team sports. The legendary 1996 US gymnastics team, known as the Magnificent Seven, won the country's first team gymnastics gold medal.

In 1999, the US women's soccer team won the World Cup in a dramatic final game. A short-lived professional women's soccer league, the Women's United Soccer Association, followed soon after. The league folded after three seasons due to lack of revenue from games and advertisements. Professional women's sports have historically received less media attention than men's sports. That, along with other ongoing gender inequality, has led some women's sports to struggle financially, especially compared with men's sports. In 2009, another league, Women's Professional Soccer, operated for three years before folding as well. As of 2018, women's professional soccer in the United States was administered by a third league, the National Women's Soccer League.

This post–Title IX era was a time for a wide range of women athletes to shine. In the 1980s and 1990s, legendary track and field athlete Jackie Joyner-Kersee won six Olympic medals, competing in the heptathlon and

Figure skater Michelle Kwan was among several female athletes who rose to fame in the 1990s, bringing attention to women in sports. Kwan won an Olympic medal in 1998 and another in 2002.

setting a long jump record. Figure skaters such as Michelle Kwan and Kristi Yamaguchi became national icons. And Mia Hamm was one of the first female soccer players to become a household name. Hamm and early WNBA greats such as Sheryl Swoopes helped usher in a new era of women stars in team sports.

CHAPTER TWO
WHAT IS THE CULTURE AROUND WOMEN AND SPORTS?

The history of women in sports shows that while women have always participated in athletics, their opportunities for participation have not been equal to men's, and many women have not been able to achieve their athletic potential. Many of the gender roles that held women back in earlier historical eras are still present today. They affect girls' and women's participation in sports, the media coverage of their achievements, and their ability to be taken seriously by society. In addition, stereotypes about women in sports are linked to cultural ideas about women's sexual desirability. Women athletes are often objectified, and women athletes in the LGBTQ (lesbian, gay, bisexual, transgender, queer or questioning) community face homophobia in the sports world.

WOMEN, SPORTS, AND GENDER ROLES

From a young age, boys and girls are given different messages about how they should look and behave. Societies communicate their expectations about what men's and women's lives should look like through cultural traditions and media. These expectations are known as gender roles.

Girls are often subtly taught by society that the competitiveness and physical strength involved in sports may be too aggressive for them. These attitudes can continue to affect female athletes throughout their careers.

Sometimes, societies send conflicting messages about gender roles for women. For example, in the United States, many books and TV shows work to give both boys and girls the message that they should follow their dreams and stay true to themselves. But other messages, sent through advertising, cultural traditions, and media, tell girls and women that their primary purposes are to attract men, get married, and raise children. Girls are often taught that being competitive, strong, or ambitious will make them less worthy and desirable and will push men away. On the flip side, men are seen as naturally aggressive, competitive, and physically dominant, and therefore more suited to sports. "[Owning sports is] part of the birthright of being male in this culture," says Mary Jo Kane, a professor and researcher of women athletes.[17] Women who choose to compete in sports are sometimes seen as threatening these gender roles. The clash between women's athleticism and their gender roles shows up in the way society treats female athletes, the way these athletes are expected to behave, and the way women athletes often see themselves.

MEDIA COVERAGE

One way the media deals with the contradictions between women athletes and traditional gender roles is by ignoring women's sports altogether. Research shows that women make up about 40 percent of all college and professional athletes but receive about 3 to 5 percent of sports coverage in the media. It is much more difficult to find a broadcast of a women's professional sports competition than a men's competition, and even extraordinary women athletes struggle to match the level of exposure that their male peers get. One study found that on the TV show *SportsCenter,* the average story about a woman athlete was half the length of a story about a male athlete.

Media coverage of women's sports varies from coverage of men's sports in content as well as quantity. Male athletes, praised for their strength or other athletic abilities, are more likely to fit into society's expectations of how a man should look and behave. For this reason, they often receive positive media coverage that focuses on the greatness of their achievements and their dominance in their fields. In contrast, physical strength and other qualities that are valued in athletes are generally not valued in women. "In order for women athletes to be taken seriously as athletes, they have to be portrayed as competent [yet this challenges] every stereotype . . . of femininity and masculinity we have in the culture," Kane says.[18] Media coverage of women is more likely to center around the athlete's body or family life. Researcher Michela Musto sums up the coverage of women's athletics as "boring."[19] While she points out that

MEDIA COVERAGE OF
WOMEN'S SPORTS

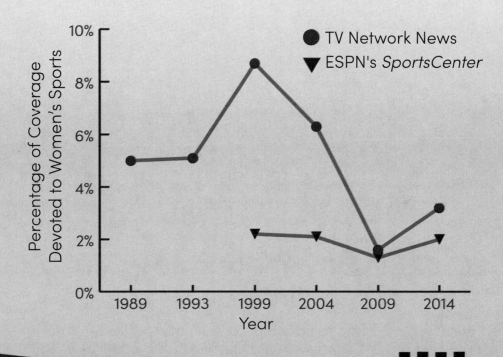

From local TV news stations to the nationally popular channel ESPN, women's sports overall receive much less media coverage than men's sports. In fact, researchers Cheryl Cooky, Michael A. Messner, and Michela Musto found that between 1989 and 2014, the overall coverage of women's sports on network news had decreased. Additionally, coverage of women's sports on ESPN's popular show *SportsCenter* decreased between 1999 and 2014. Regardless of the year, coverage of women's sports was equal to just a small percentage of men's sports coverage.

Cheryl Cooky, Michael A. Messner, and Michela Musto, "'It's Dude Time!' A Quarter Century of Excluding Women's Sports in Televised News and Highlight Shows," Communication and Sport, *June 5, 2015, p. 267.*

coverage has gotten less sexist over time, Musto believes that news media simply do not devote the same amount of attention or respect to coverage of women's sports. "There is no joking or complimenting," Musto said. "Those kinds of descriptors are missing from women's sports."[20] Some media professionals are open about their contempt for women's sports. In 2015, *Sports Illustrated* journalist Mark Mravic tweeted a short video of an exciting goal in the World Cup soccer match between England's and Norway's women's national teams. Mravic used the thrilling moment to challenge his colleague Andy Benoit's opinion that women's soccer wasn't worth watching. On Twitter, Benoit replied, "Not women's soccer . . . women's sports in general not worth watching."[21] Benoit, who as of 2018 covered the National Football League (NFL) for *Sports Illustrated,* first defended his opinion, then later apologized and deleted the tweet.

BEAUTY STANDARDS AND BODY IMAGE

The advertising and entertainment industries send strong messages to women and girls about their bodies. Women feel pressure to stay thin, avoid visible muscles that are perceived as masculine, and wear makeup and feminine clothing. Many girls in the sports world face the pressure of performing athletically while still trying to stay small and thin. However, the regular exercise that comes from participation in sports can boost girls' and women's self-esteem, mental health, and body image. Some research has found that girls and women who play sports are more likely to have a positive body image than those who do not.

The tension between beauty standards and the confidence that comes from strength and athletic ability can be difficult for female athletes to manage. One college athlete explained to researchers: "I like the way I feel when I get the muscle . . . but yet, in the back of my mind I get scared that I'm gonna get big."[22] Some female athletes respond to the double pressures of sports and social body standards by restricting their

WOMEN'S SPORTS UNIFORMS

One of the ways cultural gender roles show themselves is through clothing. Most sports have restrictions on the type of clothing players can wear during games, and it's traditional for team athletes to wear standardized uniforms. However, even within the same sport, men and women can face very different standards when it comes to dress. For example, beach volleyball is a sport played on a sandy beach with two teams of two players each. Most male beach volleyball players wear loose tank tops and long basketball-style shorts during games, in order to have freedom of movement. But until 2012, female beach volleyball players were required to wear bikinis during official games. The bikini requirement raised questions about objectification and double standards. If tight clothing was really best for playing beach volleyball, why didn't men wear it also? Was the bikini rule only in place to draw in male viewers? Others pointed out that requiring women to wear bikinis discouraged athletes who dressed modestly for religious, cultural, or personal reasons. Today, the Federation of International Volleyball gives women five choices of uniform: a bikini, a one-piece suit, a tank top paired with short shorts, a short-sleeve top and shorts just above the knee, and a long-sleeve shirt with long pants. Standards for men's dress are unchanged.

eating, which can lead to health problems. Women athletes are especially vulnerable to eating disorders, amenorrhea (lack of menstrual periods), and decreased bone density. Together, these three disorders are known as the "female athlete triad." These problems are especially common in sports such as gymnastics, figure skating, and distance running, all of which encourage athletes to keep their body weight low. Researchers estimate that between 16 and 47 percent of female elite athletes have a clinical eating disorder. Because successful athletes often have driven and disciplined personalities, disordered eating patterns can be very difficult to treat, especially in environments where being thin is considered key to success.

WOMEN'S BEHAVIOR

Traditional women's gender roles expect women to be passive, friendly, and submissive. In sports, these expectations translate to a world where women are held to higher standards of politeness and decorum in competition and in their personal lives. The All-American Girls Professional Baseball League, which toured the United States in the 1940s and 1950s, was fictionalized in the film *A League of Their Own.* One of the most famous lines comes from an exasperated male coach who tells one of his players, "There's no crying in baseball."[23] But for the women of the real league, that was not the only rule they had to follow. Players were held to strict standards of dress and behavior, from the way they styled their hair to who they could talk to off the field. The league's handbook stated:

> *Boyish bobs are not permissible and in general your hair should be well groomed at all times with longer hair preferable to short hair cuts. Lipstick should always be on.*[24]

The women of the All-American Girls Professional Baseball League were also expected to maintain a clean-cut and polite image off the baseball diamond. The league's rules emphasized that:

> *Smoking or drinking is not permissible in public places. Liquor drinking will not be permissible under any circumstances. Other intoxicating drinks in limited portions with after-game meal only, will be allowed. Obscene language will not be allowed at any time.*[25]

Those rules dictating the dress and behavior of women's baseball players may seem outdated. However, there are still parts of the sports world that tightly control the way women look and act. The NFL is the most popular professional sports league to watch in the United States. While women are not allowed to become NFL athletes, they can work as cheerleaders. NFL cheerleaders have physically demanding jobs and game schedules that match those of the players. But instead of millionaire salaries, they receive much lower wages and lack benefits such as health insurance. And many NFL teams place tight restrictions on the way cheerleaders can act both on and off the football field. The *New York Times* reported that the Oakland Raiders cheerleaders are given instructions on their body language and table manners. In 2018,

Several NFL cheerleaders have spoken out against the sexism they face in their jobs. For example, the cheerleaders' work schedules are similar to those of the professional football players they support, but the cheerleaders are paid a tiny fraction of what players earn.

New Orleans Saints cheerleader Bailey Davis was fired for posting a photo of herself in lingerie on her personal Instagram account. She filed a complaint with the federal Equal Employment Opportunity Commission, pointing out that male team employees didn't face the same restrictions on posting photos. As of August 2018, the complaint had not been resolved.

Some women athletes push back against the idea that they should look and play nice. They point out that aggression is considered more natural in male athletes. In 2009, New Mexico college soccer player

Elizabeth Lambert was suspended from her sport after she punched a player in the back, elbowed other players, and pulled a player's ponytail during a game. Lambert's behavior was unacceptable for any athlete, and she publicly apologized for her actions. But the public's reaction to the incident seemed strange to Lambert. When an ESPN commentator announced the incident on television, he said, "What is rare is when women athletes are involved in any of this [unsportsmanlike] behavior," calling the suspension "practically unbelievable."[26] Lambert pushed back against some of the media attention she received, saying "I definitely feel because I am a female it did bring about a lot more attention than if a male were to do it."[27] Lambert felt that the shocked reaction to her behavior suggested that some people didn't expect women to be emotionally invested and physically competitive soccer players. "We train very hard to reach the highest level we can get to," she said. "Sports are physical."[28]

RACIAL DISCRIMINATION IN WOMEN'S SPORTS

For much of the history of the modern world, women of color have struggled from the intersecting burdens of racial and gender prejudice. Black women in particular have had to face extra hurdles to representation and participation in sports. In the United States, most athletic events were racially segregated until the middle of the twentieth century. The first black tennis star, Ora Washington, worked as a maid in the 1920s even as she became a star on the black tennis circuit. In the 1920s, the reigning white champion, Helen Moody, refused to play a match against her.

When black women became successful in racially integrated sports, they faced accusations that they were unable or unwilling to conform to gender roles. Black women athletes were often portrayed as aggressive, unfeminine, and unfriendly. In 1957, tennis player Althea Gibson was the first black woman to become the world's top-ranked tennis player.

Because she sometimes refused interviews, Gibson was described by the press as "ungracious as a stubborn jackass."[29] The pressure that Gibson felt to represent all black people to others was stressful. "It was a strain," she said, "always trying to say and do the right thing, so that I wouldn't give people the wrong idea of what Negroes are like."[30] In the twenty-first century, tennis is still a majority-white sport at the elite level. Although Serena Williams, who is black, has been at the top of the sport for many years, she still faces many of the same pressures that Gibson did. Williams has publicly been called "manly" by sports fans and commentators, and she has been criticized for her outfits and behavior.[31] Her competitive drive and tennis ability have been portrayed as overly aggressive, with commentators referring to her "piranha mentality" and "savage strokes."[32] Williams has pushed back against these descriptions of her character. "I feel like people think I'm mean," she

> "They say African Americans have to be twice as good, especially women."[33]
> – Serena Williams, champion tennis player

explained, adding that "They say African Americans have to be twice as good, especially women. I'm perfectly OK with having to be twice as good."[33]

OBJECTIFICATION OF FEMALE ATHLETES

In 1999, the US women's soccer team faced China in the FIFA World Cup final. The game was 0-0 after thirty minutes of overtime, and each team began penalty kicks. US defender Brandi Chastain scored the final penalty goal with a high, left-footed kick. To celebrate the dramatic win, Chastain took off her jersey and kneeled in the center of the field, arms outstretched in victory. The picture of a shirtless, beaming Chastain became the iconic photo of the historic moment, landing on the front cover of three major magazines that year. Even though male soccer players had been taking their shirts off for years, some criticized Chastain's celebratory move as inappropriate and distracting. ABC News called Chastain's gesture a "strip tease" that she planned to "exploit" by endorsing sports bras for Nike.[34] Chastain did have an endorsement deal with Nike, and she later starred in a Nike commercial opposite a male athlete who played games with her, hoping to watch her take her shirt off again. For better or worse, Chastain's bra became the synonymous with her public image.

Women athletes in the public eye are often objectified by sports fans and the media. Objectification happens when human beings are treated or talked about like they are things rather than people. Female athletes face sexual objectification, or a focus on their bodies that ignores their thoughts, feelings, and athletic accomplishments. The objectification of female athletes shows up often in media coverage. Ben Wasike, a professor at University of Texas Rio Grande Valley, analyzed all *Sports Illustrated* magazine covers from 1954 to 2016. He found that men were much more likely than women to be featured on the cover of the magazine. When women athletes were featured, their photographs showed more skin, and they were more likely to be smiling and posed in sexually suggestive ways. In short, Wasike concluded that women athletes were photographed in a way that made them look sexier and less threatening to male readers.

Some women athletes feel empowered by the opportunity to show their strength and athleticism as sexy. In 2018, Olympic gymnast Aly Raisman posed nude for *Sports Illustrated*. She felt comfortable being naked for the magazine, saying, "I hope we can one day get to a point where everyone realizes that women do not have to be modest to be respected."[35] Team USA hockey forward Julie Chu was one of many athletes to pose nude for *ESPN The Magazine's* Body Issue in 2011. She enjoyed the experience, seeing the photo shoot as a way to affirm the beauty of different body types and send a positive message to young

Snowboarder Chloe Kim won a gold medal at the 2018 Winter Olympics. Shortly after, a male radio host made sexist, objectifying comments about her.

girls. "As long as you're comfortable, there's a power that comes in the picture," Chu told a newspaper.[36]

Even though naked or sexual images of women athletes can be empowering and joyful, the media often uses the sexualization of female athletes as a way to distract from or put down their accomplishments. In 2018, American snowboarder Chloe Kim won a gold medal in the Olympic women's halfpipe, finishing with an almost-perfect run and her signature back-to-back 1080 tricks. A San Francisco, California, radio host responded to her win by calling Kim a "hot piece of ass," and "fine as hell," even though he noted that Kim was seventeen years old.[37] The comments were not only insulting and inappropriate—they also took attention away from Kim's win. Media outlets began reporting not just on her gold medal but also on the rude sexual remarks a man had made about her.

For many women athletes, being sexualized in the media is a matter of compromise rather than choice. They feel that being photographed suggestively or enduring sexual comments is the price they have to pay for securing endorsements and bringing positive attention to their sport. Nicole LaVoi of the University of Minnesota's Tucker Center for Research on Girls & Women in Sport has pointed out that women athletes are not always free to choose how they are portrayed by the media. "[When] your choice is I can make money and be portrayed in sexualized ways or be portrayed and make no money," LaVoi said, "that's a difficult choice."[38]

There are also strong and athletic women whose sports require physiques that are very different from the stereotypically ideal woman's body. For these athletes, existing outside of sexualized body standards can mean struggling to find recognition and income. Sarah Robles is an American weightlifter who won three gold medals at the 2017 Weightlifting World Championships and an Olympic bronze at the 2016 Rio de Janeiro games. At the World Championships, she lifted a total of 284 kilograms, or 626.1 pounds, in the clean and jerk event. Partly because she is tall with a heavy frame, Robles struggles to find sponsorship and media support. In 2012, she was the highest-ranked weightlifter, man or woman, in the United States, but it was hard for her to find sponsors to support her grueling training schedule. "You can get that sponsorship if you're a super-built guy or a girl who looks good in a bikini. But not if you're a girl who's built like a guy," Robles said.[39] Even though Robles has to struggle with objectification by the media to gain exposure for her sport, she enjoys being a role model. "Things that used to get me bullied are the things that

> "You can get that sponsorship if you're a super-built guy or a girl who looks good in a bikini. But not if you're a girl who's built like a guy."[39]
> – Sarah Robles, Olympic weightlifter

made me to become an Olympian. Consider that when some jerk tries to tear you down," she wrote on Twitter in 2016.[40]

WOMEN, SPORTS, AND HOMOPHOBIA

Athletics can be a space for women in the LGBTQ community to challenge gender norms as well. But some LGBTQ women may feel even more pressure to conform to gender roles in sports. They may feel pressured to put in extra effort to assure others that they aren't masculine or gay. Pat Griffin, a former coach and activist against homophobia in the sports world, explains the difficult position of gay women athletes. "We have this strange sort of paradox of lesbians feeling that they need to hide, yet everyone knows that they're there," Griffin says, calling the position of gay women in sports the "glass closet."[41]

The glass closet can pressure women to keep silent about their identities, even when they face discrimination and abuse. One example comes from the world of women's basketball. The sport has a large gay female following. For decades, it was well known that many of the best college and professional women's basketball players were gay, but they were expected to never talk about it. Some coaches, such as Rene Portland of Pennsylvania State University, had official "no lesbians" policies for their basketball teams.[42] From 1980 to 2007, Portland coached the Penn State Lady Lions, a Division I team. In 1986, she spoke to the news media about her explicit bans on lesbians, telling the *Chicago Sun-Times,* "I will not have it in my program."[43] She told the newspaper that the reason for her policy was to avoid "guilt by association."[44] In other words, Portland feared that if she allowed lesbians on her team, she and all the players would be assumed to be lesbians as well. In 1991, Penn State University created a new policy banning discrimination based on sexual orientation. That same year, a *Philadelphia Inquirer* story reported that Portland did not allow homosexuality on her team. Portland stated publicly that she would abide by the policy that banned discrimination

Rene Portland resigned in 2007 from her position as women's basketball coach at this college, Pennsylvania State University. Portland had violated university policy by discriminating against players who she believed were lesbians.

based on sexual orientation. In 2006, a player named Jennifer Harris accused Portland of harassing her and trying to push her off the team. Harris said that Portland believed she was a lesbian and created a hostile environment as a result. Penn State's investigation found that Portland had violated policy and fined her $10,000. The following year, Portland resigned. Today, there are openly gay coaches and athletes in women's basketball, but many say it can still be difficult to discuss sexuality openly. Advocates like Griffin say that there is still a long way to go before homophobia in sports is a thing of the past.

SPORTS AND THE IDEA
OF WOMANHOOD

At the 1936 Olympics in Berlin, Germany, runner Helen Stephens won the women's 100-meter dash. She set a world-record time. Stephens made international headlines, but not everyone was impressed by the win. She was accused of being a man disguised as a woman. In response to the doubters, the International Olympic Committee (IOC) performed a "sex test" on Stephens by examining her genitals.[45] The test determined that Stephens was female, but she was not the last athlete accused of being too fast to be a woman.

In some cases, women's participation in sports raises controversies not only about gender roles but also about gender itself. Elite athletes who don't fit expectations of how a woman should look or perform face questions about whether they should really be considered women at all. In the 1960s, during the Cold War (1947–1991) between the United States and the Soviet Union, some people began accusing the Soviet Union of using men disguised as women to win international sports competitions. In response, the IOC began a policy of performing gender tests on women athletes. There are many general physical and biological differences between men and women's bodies. However, there is no one characteristic that always distinguishes a male body from a female one, and some bodies fall somewhere between traditional ideas of male and female. To conduct gender testing, governing bodies like the IOC must make decisions about which characteristics they think are most important to male and female identity.

In the 1960s, the IOC decided to test gender identity by requiring women athletes to strip naked in front of officials in a process known as "nude parades."[46] They checked that each woman athlete had female sex characteristics, such as breasts and female genitals. In 1968, the IOC switched to chromosome testing. Most human beings have

23 pairs of chromosomes that make up their genetic code, and one of those pairs is known as the sex chromosomes. Typically, men have one X chromosome and one Y chromosome, and women have two X chromosomes. The IOC started performing tests on female athletes to ensure that they had the standard two X chromosomes. But not all people with female sex characteristics have XX chromosomes. Some men have XX chromosomes, some women have XY, and some people have other combinations like XXY or XYY. Despite the potential for uncertainty with the test, all female Olympic athletes were required to undergo this type of gender verification until 1999.

In the 2000s, the IOC changed criteria again, from genetic to hormonal tests of gender. All human beings produce the hormone testosterone. However, since men tend to produce more of it, and because it helps develop male sex characteristics, testosterone is sometimes called a male hormone. The IOC ended mandatory sex testing in 1999, testing only in special cases. In 2016, the IOC announced that it had suspended all sex testing.

However, the International Association of Athletics Federations (IAAF), a governing body for track and field competitions, currently uses testosterone as its test of female gender. In order to compete as women, athletes must have testosterone levels that are significantly lower than those of the average man. Male elite athletes have never been subjected to gender tests to confirm their maleness and do not face any upper limits to the amount of testosterone they are allowed to have. In fact, male athletes with low levels of testosterone can apply to take steroids in order to increase the amount of the hormone in their bodies.

In 2009, Caster Semenya, a young runner from South Africa, faced the same accusations that Helen Stephens had faced more than seventy years earlier. At the 2009 World Track and Field Championships in Berlin, Semenya won her event, the 800 meters, by over two seconds. Semenya

Running star Caster Semenya won a gold medal at the 2016 Summer Olympics. In 2018, she was officially told that she could no longer compete in international track and field events because her testosterone levels were too high.

is tall, with a straight, muscular build and a low voice. After she won her event, rumors started that Semenya might not really be a woman. Semenya was used to stripping in front of fellow runners to prove to them that she was female. But after her amazing win in Berlin, the media reported that the IAAF had done other gender tests on Semenya. They found that although Semenya had external female genitalia, she did not have ovaries, which are internal female sex organs. Semenya had internal testes, which are usually external male sex organs. Semenya's body naturally produces three times as much testosterone as the average woman's. At the time, Semenya was just eighteen years old. She had grown up as a girl and identified as a woman. The international scrutiny over her gender was emotionally difficult. "I can't say to anyone how I feel or what's in my mind," Semenya said at the time.[47] Gender testing also stalled the progress of her career. Semenya was forbidden to compete as a runner for several months.

In 2015, the IAAF suspended its testosterone testing policy for two years. In 2016, Semenya won the gold medal in the 800 meters race at the Summer Olympics in Rio de Janeiro, Brazil. In April 2018, the IAAF announced that women middle-distance runners would need to keep their testosterone levels within a certain range in order to compete as women. The organization claimed in a statement that high testosterone gives women an unfair advantage in competition when it comes to sports like running. The statement stopped short of claiming that women with high testosterone are not really women. Instead, it cited research saying that high levels of testosterone in women were associated with better performance in track and field events. Women athletes like Semenya were left in an almost impossible position: The organization claimed that their natural bodies were unfair. They may not be men, but they did not belong with women unless they suppressed their hormones to levels that were considered acceptable. In June 2018, Semenya announced that she would legally challenge the IAAF's rule. "I just want to run naturally, the way I was born," Semenya said. "I am a woman and I am fast."[48] Semenya was not the only person to protest the controversial rule: Indian sprinter Dutee Chand is also fighting the regulation, and one IAAF disciplinary board member, law professor

> "I just want to run naturally, the way I was born. I am a woman and I am fast."[48]
> – Caster Semenya, track and field athlete

Steve Cornelius, resigned from his position because he disagreed with the policy.

TRANSGENDER WOMEN IN SPORTS

Gender testing regulations and their focus on low testosterone in women also affect the lives and careers of transgender women athletes. Transgender people do not identify with the gender they were assigned at birth. They often make physical and hormonal changes to their bodies so that their gender expression—the way their gender looks on the outside—matches their gender identity, or their own sense of gender. Some transgender women have testosterone levels that are similar to those of average men. Transgender women face different sets of standards for sports participation depending on their age, location, and physical features. Andraya Yearwood is a transgender girl sprinter who competes for her high school team in Connecticut. As of 2018, Connecticut was one of seventeen states that allowed high school athletes to compete as the gender they identify as, rather than the gender on their birth certificates. Yearwood has competed as a girl even though she has not taken hormone therapy. Despite Connecticut's law allowing this, Yearwood has still faced media criticism. If Yearwood were to compete in the Olympics one day, she would be required to use medical therapies to maintain a low testosterone level, unless the IAAF's rules change.

CHAPTER THREE
WHAT IS THE BUSINESS SIDE OF WOMEN AND SPORTS?

The history of Title IX, the law that requires college sports to provide equal opportunities to men and women, shows that funding is key to the development of women and girls in sports. The funding made possible by Title IX spurred huge growth in women's participation in sports and paved the way for college and professional careers. However, equality in funding opportunities at the collegiate level has not translated into financial equality in the world of professional sports.

The sports industry operates with a wide network of professionals. Athletes rely on coaches, trainers, and medical professionals to maximize performance. On the business side, agents, managers, team owners, and administrators keep the system running. Competitions are made possible by scoring officials and maintenance staff. Media employees such as journalists, commentators, and camera operators publicize athletes and explain competitions. And professional sports would not exist without the fans who pay to watch athletes play. In all of these sectors of the sports

Professional female athletes, on average, make much less money than their male counterparts. This mirrors the gender pay gap found in most industries in the United States, though the pay gap tends to be greater in sports.

business, women have less power, less money, and less representation than men do.

PAYMENT AND SPONSORSHIP FOR WOMEN ATHLETES

It's expensive to be a professional athlete. Elite competitors need equipment, supplies, and time and space to train for their sport. Professionals have to travel for training and competition, and they often have grueling schedules. Typically, athletes are paid through a combination of salaries, prize money, sponsorships, and endorsements. While women athletes make money in all of these ways, they tend to make less money than men. Professional sports is one of many industries with a gender-based pay gap. In the United States, on average, women who work full time make about 80 percent of what full-time male workers make. In the sports world, the gap between men's and women's earnings tends to be larger compared with other industries.

Salaries are yearly amounts paid to athletes by teams and other organizations. In professional sports, organizations determine the lowest and highest allowable salaries for athletes. Sports teams can choose to pay their athletes salaries on the lower or higher ends of the range. They can also recruit star athletes with signing bonuses, which are additional payments when an athlete signs on with a team. While some women do make large salaries in professional sports, their yearly earnings tend to be much lower than those of men in similar sports. As of 2017, average salaries for WNBA athletes ranged from $50,000 to $110,000. In contrast, the lowest-paid athletes in the NBA that year earned salaries of around $560,000 a year. Many WNBA athletes earn additional money by playing for overseas teams in Europe and Asia during the off-season.

Some professional sports, such as tennis and golf, work on a tournament system. Individual players enter tournaments that offer prize money to winning players. The top player in a tournament gets the largest prize, followed by the second-best player, and so on until all players are compensated. Women's professional tournaments tend to have smaller prize payouts than men's. For instance, the winner of the 2018 US Open men's golf tournament will receive more than $2 million in prize money. The 2018 Women's Open winner will get $900,000. This difference continues for other players in the tournament. The twentieth-place finisher at the men's tournament will make slightly more money than the woman who places tenth at her competition. For golf star Stacy Lewis, who plays with the Ladies' Professional Golf Association (LPGA) the pay gap is "pretty frustrating."[49] "We're doing the same thing and the only difference is the TV numbers and the TV ratings," Lewis explained. "That's really it."[50]

Sponsorships are money given to athletes to cover training and living costs. Most sponsors are corporations that give money to athletes in exchange for the opportunity to advertise their brands with the athletes.

> "We're doing the same thing and the only difference is the TV numbers and the TV ratings. That's really it."[50]
> – Stacy Lewis, professional golfer

Companies that sell athletic clothing and equipment are especially eager to pay professional athletes to wear and advertise their brands. Sportswear brand Nike, for example, offered sponsorships to fifty-four of the world's 100 highest-paid athletes in 2018. These sponsorships can vary from offers of free company products to multimillion-dollar contracts to appear in advertisements. While some women do get these sponsorships, the money primarily goes to male athletes. According to the Women in Sports Foundation, between 2011 and 2013, women's sports sponsorships made up just 0.4 percent of total sponsorship deals.

Endorsements are advertisements that use an athlete's popularity to sell a product that may or may not be directly related to sports. In endorsements, athletes recommend a product, encouraging their fans and admirers to buy it. Corporate sponsors may or may not require their athletes to do endorsements in exchange for the sponsorships they receive. Women lag far behind men in endorsement deals. This is not because women don't purchase sportswear or other goods. Women are responsible for up to 70 to 80 percent of all global consumer purchases. Instead, experts say that the gap in endorsement deals is due to gender expectations. Male athletes are more likely to be considered enviable. According to marketer Kevin Adler, "You'd be hard-pressed to find a popular male athlete who doesn't also have physicality and sex appeal."[51]

According to this logic, male athletes' opinions of products are worthwhile because all male athletes are automatically attractive. Women athletes, however, must be considered conventionally beautiful as well as athletic in order to score big deals.

Combined, these income factors add up to profound differences in the amount of money that male and female athletes make from sports. In June 2018, the business magazine *Forbes* published its annual list of the world's 100 highest-paid athletes. All 100 athletes listed were men. The year before, one woman, Serena Williams, made the list. Williams has been one of the most dominant players in women's tennis for more than two decades. She has won twenty-three Grand Slam singles titles, more than any other person in the modern era of tennis, with her twenty-third title earned in 2017. She won her fourth Olympic gold medal in 2016. Williams has been called the greatest athlete in America and of all time. In 2017, Williams placed fifty-first on *Forbes'* list of the world's highest-paid athletes, with a yearly income of $27 million. She was the only woman on the list that year and was not on the list in 2018 due to taking time off while pregnant. Comparatively, Roger Federer, a tennis star who has twenty Grand Slam singles, along with one gold and one silver Olympic medal, ranked fourth highest-paid on that same *Forbes* list in 2017, with an income of $64 million.

FIGHTING AGAINST THE PAY GAP

Some women's sports teams have pushed back against what they see as payment discrimination. In 2016, the US women's soccer team sued the United States Soccer Federation. The team pointed out that even though some women soccer players earn higher salaries than some male

"In this day and age, it's about equality. It's about equal rights. It's about equal pay."[52]
– Hope Solo, professional soccer player

Tennis star Serena Williams is widely considered one of the greatest athletes of all time. She was the only woman on a list of the world's 100 highest-paid athletes in 2017.

players do, overall pay for women was about a quarter of men's pay. US women's soccer player Hope Solo has described pay equality as part of the struggle for gender equality. "In this day and age, it's about equality. It's about equal rights. It's about equal pay," Solo said.[52] In 2017, the team reached an agreement with the US Soccer Federation. The deal gave them higher pay but stopped short of achieving total pay equality with men. The deal was set to last through 2021, at which point the team would have another chance to negotiate.

PAYMENT AND PERFORMANCE

Why are women athletes paid less than men are? According to analysts, the answer is that viewers are simply less interested in watching women play. The public prefers to watch men's sports and idolize male athletes. Also, since women's athletics get much less media exposure than men's, their events simply don't present the same moneymaking opportunities for companies. Some viewers may not even know that women's professional leagues exist in a given sport. "They just aren't aware of it," said professional hockey player Kaleigh Fratkin.[53]

This argument traps women athletes in a cycle that is difficult to escape. Without media exposure, women's sports have fewer opportunities to make money. Without money to support their training, female athletes struggle to devote the time and energy they need to reach their full potential in their sport. And without female athletes at the top of their game, it's even more difficult for women's sports to get exposure in the media.

The story of National Pro Fastpitch, a professional softball league, helps demonstrate how the cycle of underfunding and underexposure stalls women's athletic careers. College women's softball is a popular spectator sport. Often, the Women's College World Series of softball draws a bigger TV audience than the biggest college men's baseball events. Women in NCAA programs can count on Title IX funding to help them access resources and develop their skills. After college, however, it is almost unheard of for a woman to make a living as a professional softball player.

The 2017 documentary *Burn the Ships* tells the story of the 2015 season of the Akron Racers softball team. The team was based in Akron,

Women's college softball is generally more popular than men's college baseball. But female professional softball players are paid much less than the men playing Major League Baseball.

Ohio, and was the oldest of five professional women's softball teams in the United States. The Racers were funded by private donors and managed by just one woman. The team manager, Joey Arrietta, took care of updating the team's changing rooms and facilities, buying uniforms and equipment, and even picking her players up from the airport. The team, along with the rest of the league, struggled to make money through ticket sales and advertising. Unlike men's professional baseball teams, which earned millions of dollars in revenue by selling the TV rights to their games, the National Pro Fastpitch league had to pay up to $50,000 to broadcast a softball game on CBS Sports.

Also unlike men's baseball players, who received year-round salaries, the 2015 players of the Akron Racers were only paid for the three summer months that they spent playing for the team. Most lived in other cities and worked jobs that could give them summer time off and enough money to survive on for the rest of the year. They trained when they could and worked on keeping fit in their spare time. The documentary profiles one talented former player, center fielder Lisa Modglin. Modglin had to balance her career on the team with her job as an accountant. For several seasons, she sacrificed three months of her regular job in order to pursue her passion for softball. "Not that accounting is bad," Modglin said in 2010, "but this is so much better than sitting in an office right now."[54] By the time she was twenty-seven, however, Modglin was retired from professional softball, mostly for financial reasons. "At the end of the day, I make more money in an accounting firm working full time," Modglin said. "It takes a little bit of a toll on you."[55]

In February 2018, the struggling Akron Racers were reformed as the Cleveland Comets, with new management and players. Arrietta left the team as manager, and the team was remade with a mix of American and international players. As of July 2018, the National Pro Fastpitch league included five teams, three of which were based in the United States. The new league included one team in Beijing, China, and another in Australia. These changes were designed to bring more money to the professional league, but professional softball still may not survive in the United States. National Pro Fastpitch Commissioner Cheri Kempf believes that businesses are missing a huge opportunity to sponsor and support

"There exists a consistency in corporate America to turn away from women's sports, in spite of the fact that it makes business sense."[56]
– Cheri Kempf, commissioner of National Pro Fastpitch

women's softball. "There exists a consistency in corporate America to turn away from women's sports, in spite of the fact that it makes business sense," Kempf said. "I don't expect corporate America to step up and make lemonade out of lemons. I think we're lemonade."[56]

WOMEN IN SPORTS MEDIA

Like corporate sponsorships, sports media coverage also focuses disproportionately on male athletes. This may be related to the fact that sports media coverage is overwhelmingly created by male writers, editors, newscasters, and other professionals. The Institute for Diversity and Ethics in Sport (TIDES) issues reports with letter grades for race and gender diversity among editorial staff in sports newsrooms. In 2018, TIDES gave sports media a grade of "F" for gender diversity in hiring. Only 17.9 percent of staff at the seventy-five newspapers and websites that TIDES researched were women, including just 11.5 percent of reporters.

Women sports reporters and media personalities can face the same objectification that female athletes do. A Google search for "female sports reporter" returns lists of professional women ranked by their physical appearance. In some cases, women professionals in sports media face sexual harassment and professional harassment. Unsafe workplaces for women media professionals can cause great damage to women's careers and overall health.

In 1990, twenty-six-year-old sports journalist Lisa Olson was interviewing a group of NFL players in a Boston locker room. A group of players began sexually harassing her by making obscene comments and asking her to touch them sexually. Olson filed a harassment lawsuit and won. But she had to move to Australia to escape threats from angry fans. "She went through hell," Olson's friend and fellow sports journalist Joanne Gerstner said.[57] Eventually, Olson returned to the United States and resumed her sportswriting career. She now gives advice to other women in sports who deal with sexual harassment and physical assault from

MARKETING TO FEMALE NFL FANS

Women make up a large percentage of ticket sales and audience numbers for the NFL. Despite the large market of female fans, sports teams and organizations often struggle to market to women. In 2015, the Tampa Bay Buccaneers football team created a channel specifically for female fans. One event specifically marketed to women advertised makeup and style tips as well as ways to integrate a love of football into "interests . . . such as home entertaining."[1] The channel was widely mocked and criticized by female fans. They found the marketers' focus on makeup instead of football to be condescending. Today, NFL marketers are working to leave behind a stereotypically feminine approach to marketing to women, offering the same products to fans of any gender instead of giving women more stereotypically feminine products. The NFL has tried to connect to female football fans by acknowledging the problem of players' violence against women and committing to increasing opportunities for women in the sports business. In 2018, the NFL held its third annual Women's Summit, a forum to discuss the issues of women in football. While female sportswriters described some of the summit's panels as "promising," the event drew criticism for failing to take concerns about sexism seriously.[2] One journalist reported that attendees were given cookbooks as favors, and another pointed out that only men were invited to give the summit's opening remarks.

1. Quoted in Cindy Boren, "Bucs Try to Help the Ladies Understand Football and Instead Infuriate Them," Washington Post, August 6, 2015. www.washingtonpost.com
2. Melissa Jacobs, "NFL's Women's Summit Misses the Mark," The Football Girl, February 2, 2018. www.thefootballgirl.com.

players and staff. In a 2017 article, Olson connected her experience with that of Lisa Guerrero, a TV announcer who was humiliated on camera by colleagues who joked that she slept with the athletes she interviewed. Olson and Guerrero agree that women must continue sharing stories of discrimination in order to change the sexist attitudes surrounding women in sports media. "There's one saving grace in all of this," Guerrero said. "We're finally talking about it."[58]

Some younger journalists are hopeful that these attitudes will change. Mina Kimes is a senior writer at *ESPN The Magazine*. She sometimes deals with men who doubt her sports knowledge or reporting ability.

But Kimes chooses to see other people's prejudices as a source of strength. As she explained in 2014, "If a man chooses to react with surprise or condescension . . . I've always just felt that it's to their disadvantage and not mine."[59]

> "If a man chooses to react with surprise or condescension . . . I've always just felt that it's to their disadvantage and not mine."[59]
>
> – *Mina Kimes, senior writer at ESPN The Magazine*

WOMEN COACHES AND ADMINISTRATORS

In the world of youth sports, women coaches are relatively rare. In 2015, the Sports and Fitness Industry Association found that only 27 percent of youth sports coaches were women. At the college level, the percentage of women's sports coaches actually declined after Title IX. Before the law was enacted, 90 percent of college women's sports were coached by women. Title IX increased the number of opportunities and pay level for women's sports coaches, which made more men interested in the jobs. As a result, by 2014, only 43 percent of women's college teams were coached by women. In professional sports, women coaches are even more rare. In 2018, half of all WNBA head coaches were women. However, as of April 2018, there were no female head coaches of any men's professional sports teams. A small handful of women have found assistant coaching positions in the NBA. The NFL employed one female line judge as of 2018.

Colleges and universities are not required to pay equal salaries to men's and women's sports coaches, and coaches of women's teams tend to be paid less than men's coaches are. Despite these obstacles, some women have managed to accomplish extraordinary coaching careers. Pat Summitt was a college basketball player and a 1976 Olympic silver medalist in women's basketball. She spent thirty-eight seasons

MLB'S FEMALE GROUNDSKEEPERS

Baseball diamonds need a great deal of maintenance to stay neat and ready for play. Groundskeepers—the professionals who take care of the grass and field—play a vital role in baseball. They roll dirt, cut and water grass, repair damage caused by players, and protect the grounds from weather. It's common for groundskeepers to work fifteen hours a day during the baseball season. There have only been two female groundskeepers in the history of Major League Baseball (MLB). Heather Nabozny, who works for the Detroit Tigers, became the first female MLB groundskeeper in 1999. She grew up with a father who worked in the lawn care business and entered the baseball world in her twenties. The Baltimore Orioles' Nicole Sherry followed in Nabozny's footsteps in 2007, after a career in minor league baseball. Both women acknowledge that battling weather and nature to keep their fields perfect can be challenging. But they feel supported by their teams and love what they do. "This is my dream job," Sherry said.

Quoted in Pat Stoetzer, "Baseball: For Orioles' Groundskeeper Sherry, 'This Is My Dream Job,'" Carroll County Times, July 22, 2017. www.carrollcountytimes.com.

coaching the University of Tennessee's Lady Volunteers basketball team. Summitt, who died in 2016, is widely considered the most successful Division I women's basketball coach in history. She coached 1,098 winning games and is credited with bringing attention and respect to women's college basketball. By 2006, she became the first women's basketball coach to earn more than $1 million in one season. Summitt became one of the few women's coaches in college basketball to earn more than her men's counterpart. The historic raise put her just above Tennessee's men's coach at the time, Bruce Pearl. Pearl, who as of 2018 had coached 301 wins in a fourteen-year career, also earned more than $1 million that season.

In addition to coaching staff, the sports industry relies heavily on administrators and officials who schedule games, manage finances, represent athletes, and make sure that competitions run smoothly. Traditionally, this area of the sports industry has been male-dominated as well. In the most prestigious college and professional sports organizations, women make up less than 10 percent of lead executives. However, some women are carving out influential careers in sports administration.

Michele Roberts is the executive director of the National Basketball Players Association, a union for NBA players. She advocates for the interests of professional basketball players. She is the first woman to lead a professional sports union. Roberts is a former lawyer who earns a minimum annual salary of $1.2 million at the organization. Roberts, who is black, is proud to be a role model for women, especially women of color, who seek careers in professional sports. She takes the responsibility of being a groundbreaking woman seriously, and she has warned her colleagues that it's a mistake to ignore or diminish her. "My past is littered with the bones of men who were foolish enough to think I was someone they could sleep on," Roberts said.[60] In 2018, *Forbes* named Roberts the most powerful woman in the sports business.

> "My past is littered with the bones of men who were foolish enough to think I was someone they could sleep on."[60]
> – *Michele Roberts, executive director of the National Basketball Players Association*

CHAPTER FOUR

WHAT IS THE FUTURE OF WOMEN AND SPORTS?

Picabo Street, an Olympic alpine skier in the 1990s and early 2000s, once said that "to uncover your true potential you must first find your own limits and then you have to have the courage to blow past them."[61] The climate has never been ideal for women in sports. Female athletes face cultural and financial obstacles to meeting their true potential. But women athletes and their supporters keep pushing past limits to discover the potential of women and sports.

Today, new opportunities are opening up in the world of sports. There are organizations that recognize the vital role that sports can play in all women's lives, and they are working hard to offer girls and women more ways to play. Scholars, historians, and activists hope to change society's ideas about gender roles. They are looking to raise awareness of the accomplishments of women athletes so that women at all levels of sports have the freedom and respect they need to reach their full potential.

But it's not just culture and business practices that have the potential to change. Sports themselves are evolving. With new sports and new

There are several organizations working to study gender inequality in sports and to improve opportunities for women in sports. Much of this effort goes toward advocating for enforcement of Title IX, which requires high schools and colleges to provide equal sports opportunities to men and women.

ways of playing come new ideas about what women's sports are and what women are capable of.

TITLE IX ENFORCEMENT AND REFORM

Although Title IX is more than forty years old, data suggest that more than one-fourth of public high schools still devote disproportionate money and resources to boys' sports. Legal and nonprofit organizations such as the

National Women's Law Center continue the work of monitoring Title IX compliance and advocating for change. In 1974, tennis legend Billie Jean King started the Women's Sports Foundation, which works to advocate for Title IX enforcement in education programs across the country. The foundation has produced more than forty research studies on how to promote gender equality in sports and highlight the positive effect of sports on girls' and women's lives. The nonprofit Legal Aid at Work helps hold public schools accountable for offering equal opportunities for girls to play sports. It offers advice to people looking to file Title IX claims, and it advocates for state and federal legislation designed to strengthen gender equality in sports.

Title IX legislation is designed to guard against gender-based discrimination in every area of academic life, not just sports. Women and girls who face sexual harassment or are sexually assaulted at school can file Title IX complaints against their abusers. But for female athletes who have been sexually abused by coaches, authority figures, or other players, Title IX has not always served as a protection. In 2014, Michigan State University student Amanda Thomashaw filed a Title IX complaint against gymnastics team doctor Larry Nassar, alleging that he had sexually abused her during a medical exam. Michigan State investigated the claim and cleared Nassar of any misconduct. The university also gave Thomashaw an edited version of its report, which omitted key information about the investigation. Later, more than 150 amateur and professional gymnasts came forward to accuse Nassar of similar sexual abuse. In January 2018, Nassar was sentenced to 175 years in prison after being found guilty of seven counts of criminal sexual abuse. Because of the structure of Title IX, Michigan State was allowed to handle Thomashaw's complaint internally rather than hiring an outside investigator or contacting law enforcement. Critics of this part of the law believe that law enforcement, not schools, should have jurisdiction over investigating sexual misconduct.

THE NEXT GENERATION OF GIRLS IN SPORTS

Young girls and boys tend to participate in sports at roughly equal rates. By age fourteen, however, girls drop out of sports at twice the rate of boys. This gap in sports participation continues into adulthood. For some women, there is still a struggle to even have the opportunity to play sports. Research shows that girls from low-income families are far less likely than other children to participate in sports throughout their lifetimes. Tom Farrey, director of the nonprofit Aspen Institute's Sports and Society Program, said, "Sports in America have separated into sport-haves and have-nots."[62] Sports participation can be expensive for children, and wealthy families are increasingly training their children in private,

"Sports in America have separated into sport-haves and have-nots."[62]
– Tom Farrey, director of the nonprofit Aspen Institute's Sports and Society Program

rather than public, sports programs. In June 2018, women's soccer star Hope Solo criticized US youth soccer for becoming too expensive for many American kids to play. She pointed out that when children lack the opportunity to start out in sports, college and professional teams lose out on talent.

In the past few decades, nonprofit and international organizations have worked to help girls and women increase their participation in sports. The Women's Sports Foundation provides grants to underprivileged girls so they can participate in sports. It also offers scholarships to female college athletes. Soccer star Mia Hamm's foundation also helps fund opportunities for girls and young women to grow in sports. Local organizations such as Chicago's Girls in the Game help increase girls' access to sports by offering all-girl sports after-school programs and camps to help the next generation of girls grow as athletes and people.

RECLAIMING "PLAY LIKE A GIRL"

"You play like a girl" is an insult that many boys and girls grew up hearing on the playground. In baseball, a young player who throws with poor technique is sometimes teased by other kids for "throwing like a girl." Using "like a girl" as an insult is a way of associating inexperience with girls and women.

Some organizations are working to change the phrase "You play like a girl" from an insult into a source of empowerment. A nonprofit organization called Play Like A Girl helps girls access sports and STEM education as a way of preparing them for successful careers. In 2017, the US Olympic Committee asked female athletes to share their ideas of what it means to "play like a girl." Some women athletes shared childhood experiences of not being allowed to play with the boys. Luge athlete Erin Hamlin remembered being self-conscious of her muscles growing up. Today, however, she feels proud of her strength. "To me, to 'play like a girl' means to embrace the strength your body and mind has, whatever that looks like," she said.

Quoted in Lisa Costantini, "9 U.S. Olympians Share Their Definition of 'Play Like A Girl,'" Team USA, March 23, 2017. www.teamusa.org.

SPORTS AT EVERY AGE

Adult women are much less likely to participate in amateur sports than adult men. About 35 percent of adult American men play sports for fun, whereas only about 16 percent of women do the same. This gap persists even though research shows that playing sports can help people stay physically and mentally healthy as they age. Some women who grew up in a time before Title IX offered more opportunities to female athletes have been able to find joy in sports later in life. The National Senior Games Association, founded in 1985, tries to encourage older people to play sports by hosting competitions for male and female athletes older than fifty. The 2017 Senior Games in Birmingham, Alabama, hosted more than 10,000 athletes.

CHANGING THE IMAGE

It's Mary Jo Kane's job to analyze media coverage of women athletes. She knows how the media ignores and devalues women's contributions to the sports world. One common argument states that the sexualization and objectification of women athletes helps bring attention to women's sports. But Kane has noticed something interesting about a handful of women's competitions: When women athletes are covered the same way men are, viewers tune in. She points out that the NCAA's March Madness women's basketball tournament gets huge numbers of fans, both in stadiums and watching TV. "Coverage of the women's Final Four," Kane wrote, "bears a remarkable resemblance to that of the men's—a focus on great traditions, conference rivalries (Duke vs. North Carolina), legendary coaches (Pat Summitt vs. Geno Auriemma)—and, most important, showcasing sportswomen as physically gifted, mentally tough, grace-under-pressure athletes."[63] Cheryl Cooky, a professor at Purdue University, agrees that treating women athletes the same way men are treated is key to changing media narratives and "shifting the cultural perceptions of gender roles and expectations."[64] A few committed professionals are working to do just that, but investing in women's sports media is still financially risky. In 2016, two female entrepreneurs launched Excelle Sports, one of the first websites devoted to serious, year-round coverage of all women's sports. The website folded in December 2017 due to lack of funding. Sports giant ESPN has a women's sports initiative called espnW, but it's still mostly confined to digital, rather than TV, coverage. Respectful, widely publicized media coverage of women's athletics is still rare.

On the business side, organizations such as the Institute for Sport and Social Justice have programs designed to share the experiences of women, especially women of color, working in the sports industry. The institute began the Invisible Women in Sport conference as a way to celebrate the contributions of women of color in the sports industry and to "[generate] a discussion of academic and career pathways to encourage and improve opportunities for women of color in sports," according to its website.[65] The institute publishes a podcast in which prominent women of color in sports can share their experiences and challenges with others

Many women love to watch sports on TV. However, sports media continue to cater to male fans and to cover men's sports more than women's.

in the business. Women who work in sports media and at events have professional development organizations such as the Association for Women in Sports Media, Women in Sports and Events (WISE), and the Alliance of Women Coaches. The Association for Women in Sports Media sponsors an annual conference and an internship program that works to place aspiring female sports journalists and broadcasters in paid summer jobs. The Alliance of Women Coaches offers mentorship and resources for women in the coaching field. By advocating for female athletes and other women in sports, all of these organizations are shaping the future of sports for women.

UNITING FOR EQUAL PAY AND REPRESENTATION

Athletes and activists point out that male athletes can be key allies in the fight for equal representation and equal pay in sports. In 2007, sisters and tennis stars Venus Williams and Serena Williams helped close the gap between men's and women's pay at the Wimbledon tennis tournament. In 2018, the sisters called on men to help raise awareness about ongoing pay gaps in women's sports. "We need females supporting it and men advocating for it," Serena Williams said.[66] In 2017, female professional ice hockey players ended a negotiation with the USA Hockey governing body over better salaries and treatment. The women players were able to negotiate increases in salary from about $1,000 a month to $3,000 to $4,000 a month. While these payment amounts were still lower than what male hockey players received, the women players also negotiated for benefits such as business class transportation, travel stipends, and disability insurance. All these benefits had been awarded to the men's team earlier. The US women's hockey team had threatened to boycott the International Ice Hockey Federation world championships unless they achieved their goals in the negotiations. The US men's hockey team issued a public statement in support of the women's team. "Having these men jump onboard showed what it means when men are secure, professional athletes," US women's team captain Meghan Duggan said.[67] The men's gesture helped show the power of cooperation between men and women in sports.

The inequality surrounding women's participation in sports, both as players and spectators, is recognized as a global human rights issue. The United Nations Educational, Scientific, and Cultural Organization (UNESCO) recognizes that "gender ratios in sport remain highly unequal around the globe."[68] As a result, the United Nations has included "equal opportunities to play, equal pay, and equal representation" for women in sports as part of its 2030 Sustainable Development Goals.[69] In 2018, the

International Olympic Committee approved and published twenty-five recommendations from its Gender Equality Review Project. The recommendations are meant to ensure gender balance among Olympic athletes, coaches, and officials. They aim to make sure men and women are treated fairly in competition and are given equal resources in future Olympic games.

MEN AND WOMEN COMPETING TOGETHER

Not all sports follow the traditional division between men's and women's competition. Ice skating and ice dancing both feature events in which men and women work together in pairs. Tennis and badminton both have long traditions of mixed-doubles games. In these games, two teams of one man and one woman each play against each other. However, mixed-gender sports competitions are overall less popular than competitions between athletes of the same sex. But supporters of mixed-doubles sports say that they are underrated. "There's equality in sports, enthusiasm, men and women competing together," tennis fan Wayne Bryan said. "It just doesn't get the attention it deserves."[70] The 2020 Summer Olympics will offer more mixed events in track and field, swimming, table tennis, and triathlon.

Most mixed-gender sports require an equal number of men and women on each team. But a very small number of sports do not have gender restrictions at all. Equestrian events, such as horse riding, do not separate competitions by gender. These sports are known as gender neutral because men and women are allowed to compete together with no restrictions on the number of men and women per team. In the future, more sports may move toward gender neutrality. This includes ski jumping, which opened to women at the Olympic level in 2014 after years of lobbying by female ski jumpers. Shortly after the sport was added to the Olympics, it became clear that men's and women's top distances

Ski jumping is one sport that may become mixed-gender in the future because of similarities in men's and women's competition records. Women were first allowed to compete in ski jumping at the Olympic level in 2014.

were extremely similar. Bias against female ski jumpers held women back in the past, but gender neutrality could be in the sport's future.

Long-distance yachting is a mixed-gender sport, but the future of this is up for debate. The Volvo Ocean Race is an around-the-world boating race that covers more than 45,000 nautical miles (83,340 km). The race takes months to complete. In 2015, the winning team finished the race in just over 146 days. In 2017, the Volvo Ocean Race changed its rule book so that yachting crews with at least two women were allowed to have more crew members than all-male teams. Partly as a result of this rule, the 2018 race was the first in which each of the seven teams had women on board. The winning team included three women. Although women sailors believe that the rule shift represents progress for them, they hope that it won't be necessary one day. Navigator Libby Greenhalgh wants to see an all-female crew perform well in the race. "I still think women have to go and do the next race as a team themselves and go out and perform and prove it," she said.[71]

EXPANDING THE FIELD

Athletic competitions require a huge variety of physical and mental skills. There is no one measure of what makes a body athletic. Many traditional sports rely on skills such as running speed, muscle strength, and muscular endurance for success. Conventional wisdom says that on average, men are faster and stronger than women and that the most athletic men will always outperform the most athletic women. But history and science tell a more complicated story.

It is true that in sports that measure strength and speed, men tend to perform better than women. In running and swimming competitions, men's world records are about 10 percent faster than women's records. In weightlifting, the difference between men and women hovers closer to 36 percent. The difference between male and female records is called the *performance gap*. The average difference in muscle tone between male and female athletes is called the *muscle gap*. Over time, both of these gaps have gotten smaller. There is some evidence that in the distant past, women may have had much stronger upper bodies than they tend to have now. But can the strength and speed gender gaps ever close completely? Some people argue that because women have faced so many barriers to participation and success in sports, they simply need more time and resources to catch up to men's performances. They point to the history of men's and women's sports as evidence that it is possible to close these gaps. The human body hasn't changed in the past century, but ideas about men's and women's athletic abilities certainly

THE WOMEN OF FREE DIVING

Free divers are extreme athletes who train their bodies to go without air for minutes in order to swim hundreds of feet below the ocean's surface. In some ways, free diving is a new sport. It is not recognized by the Olympics. The official international organization for free diving, called Association Internationale pour le Développement de l'Apnée (AIDA), was established in 1992. But women have been practicing the art of free diving for thousands of years. In Japan and South Korea, free diving is an ancient and exclusively female profession. Without scuba or any other artificial breathing equipment, Japanese divers, known as *ama*, and Korean divers, or *haenyeo*, plunge down 50 feet (15 m) or more into the ocean. There, they collect seafood and pearl oysters to bring to the surface and sell. Some people believe that women were chosen to become divers partly because they have higher body fat percentages than men on average, which may help them withstand cold waters. Today, AIDA keeps track of women's and men's free diving records separately. Tanya Streeter, a free diver from the Cayman Islands, once held the world record, regardless of gender, for a No Limits Apnea dive. As of 2018, she still held the world record among female No Limits Apnea divers. In No Limits Apnea, divers descend into the ocean using a weighted sled and hold an inflatable bag to come back up. In 2002, Streeter dove 525 feet (160 m) in a single breath.

have. Many current women's world records would have been men's records a few generations ago. For example, as of 2018, Ethiopian runner Almaz Ayana holds the women's world record in the 10,000-meter event with a time of twenty-nine minutes and just over seventeen seconds. In 1952, male runner Emil Zapotek won gold at the Helsinki Olympics with a 10,000-meter run time of twenty-nine minutes and seventeen seconds. However, others point to the persistence of these strength and speed gaps as proof that men, as a group, will always maintain some athletic advantage, despite the progress that women have made in the past few decades.

No one knows for sure why the performance gap exists. But the dominance of men in many popular sports can be partly explained by the fact that, historically, sports have been organized around competitions designed by men, for men. New frontiers in sports are challenging traditional ideas about whether the sports that are popular today truly

There are measured differences, or gaps, in the natural athletic abilities of men and women. However, research shows that, over many years, women in sports have started becoming faster and stronger.

represent all types of athleticism. One overlooked dimension of sports is the power of women's endurance.

The English Channel is the 21-mile (33.8-km) stretch of ocean that separates the United Kingdom from mainland Europe. On August 24, 1875, a British man named Captain Matthew Webb became the first recorded person to swim across the English Channel. He left Dover, England, and arrived on the shores of Calais, France, twenty-two hours later. Webb became a celebrity, and others tried to match his achievement. More than fifty years later, a nineteen-year-old woman named Gertrude Ederle decided to make the swim as well. Ederle was already a swimming phenomenon with three Olympic medals to her name when she decided to make the trip. She greased her body with sheep fat and sang to herself in the water to help the time go by. On her first attempt, she was pulled out of the water because spectators thought she was drowning. (She insisted it was just a rest.) On her second try, after fourteen hours, Ederle made it to the shores of France. She beat the standing world record by almost two hours. She spoke about her achievement in a matter-of-fact way, telling the *New York Times*, "I knew it could be done, it had to be done, and I did it."[72]

Since Ederle's historic swim, thousands of people have swum the English Channel. The current world-record holder for the fastest swim is a man. However, researchers have noticed something interesting about female and male participants in ultra-long-distance sports such as ocean swimming and ultramarathons—while top speed records tend to belong to men, the average woman competitor in these events performs faster than the average male competitor. For now, evidence suggests that women may have some advantage in sports that require the type of long-distance endurance that athletes like Ederle needed. These long-distance sports will continue to grow and change, giving women more chances to write new chapters in sports history.

MOVING FORWARD

In June 2018, Ashima Shiraishi, the champion rock climber, announced that she was moving to Japan. The move, she said, would help her train for the 2020 Summer Olympics in Tokyo. The Olympics' rock climbing event will include three disciplines: bouldering, sport, and speed. Like her competitors, Shiraishi will compete in all three and hope to medal based on her combined scores. She said the move to Japan would also help her "enjoy the abundance of rocks spread out all over the country."[73] As a young athlete in a growing sport, Shiraishi does not know what the future holds for her. For now, she is prepared to deal with the challenges of new rocks in a new country. Like the courageous and creative women athletes who came before her, Shiraishi has never been afraid of problems.

SOURCE NOTES

INTRODUCTION: THE HORIZON PROBLEM

1. Brett Lowell, *Instagram*, March 22, 2016. www.instagram.com.

2. Ashima Shiraishi, "Get Back on the Rock," *The Players' Tribune*, February 9, 2017. www.theplayerstribune.com.

3. Quoted in Sara Coughlin, "Ashima Shiraishi Wants You to Stop Saying She's Good 'For a Girl,'" *Refinery29*, April 17, 2018. www.refinery29.com.

4. Quoted in Jessica Holland, "At Just 17, Ashima Shiraishi Is Climbing's Fastest-Rising Star," *Huck*, April 17, 2018. www.huckmag.com.

5. Quoted in Mandy Oaklander, "This 15-Year-Old Girl Could Be the Best Rock Climber Ever," *Time*, June 3, 2016. www.time.com.

CHAPTER 1: WHAT IS THE HISTORY BEHIND WOMEN AND SPORTS?

6. Allen Guttman, *Sports: The First Five Millennia*. Amherst, MA: University of Massachusetts Press, 2004, p. 119.

7. Quoted in Jean O'Reilly and Susan K. Cahn, *Women and Sports in the United States*. Boston, MA: Northeastern University Press, 2007, p. 58.

8. Quoted in L.A. Jennings, *She's a Knockout!: A History of Women in Fighting Sports*. Lanham, MD: Rowman & Littlefield, 2015, p. 20.

9. Quoted in Guttman, *Sports: The First Five Millennia*, p. 125.

10. Quoted in O'Reilly and Cahn, *Women and Sports in the United States*, p. 54.

11. Quoted in Larry Schwartz, "More Info on Babe Didrikson," *ESPN Classic*, November 19, 2003. www.espn.com.

12. Quoted in Schwartz, "More Info on Babe Didrikson."

13. Jim Sargent, *We Were the All-American Girls*. Jefferson, NC: McFarland & Company, Inc., Publishers, 2013, p. 175.

14. Eoghan Macguire, "Althea Gibson: The 'She-Ro' Who Inspired Tennis to Change," *CNN*, September 2, 2014. www.cnn.com.

15. Quoted in O'Reilly and Cahn, *Women and Sports in the United States*, p. 348.

16. Quoted in O'Reilly and Cahn, *Women and Sports in the United States*, p. 41.

CHAPTER 2: WHAT IS THE CULTURE AROUND WOMEN AND SPORTS?

17. Quoted in *Playing Unfair: The Media Image of the Female Athlete*. Directed by Sut Jhally, Media Education Foundation, 2002.

18. Quoted in *Playing Unfair: The Media Image of the Female Athlete*.

19. Quoted in Ian Chaffee, "Forget About Sexism: Now TV Coverage of Women's Sports Is Just Plain Boring," *USC News*, September 12, 2017. news.usc.edu.

20. Quoted in Chaffee, "Forget About Sexism: Now TV Coverage of Women's Sports Is Just Plain Boring."

21. Quoted in Timothy Burke, "Dopey *Sports Illustrated* Writer: Women's Sports Aren't Worth Watching," *Deadspin*, June 22, 2015. www.deadspin.com.

22. Quoted in O'Reilly and Cahn, *Women and Sports in the United States*, p. 87.

23. *A League of Their Own*. Directed by Penny Marshall, performances by Geena Davis, Tom Hanks, Madonna, and Lori Petty, Parkway Productions, 1992.

24. Quoted in O'Reilly and Cahn, *Women and Sports in the United States*, p. 59.

25. Quoted in O'Reilly and Cahn, *Women and Sports in the United States*, p. 60.

26. "Elizabeth Lambert of New Mexico Lobos Suspended," *YouTube*, November 6, 2009. www.youtube.com.

27. Quoted in Katy Kelleher, "Violence In Sports: Suspended Soccer Player Speaks Out," *Jezebel*, November 18, 2009. www.jezebel.com.

28. Quoted in Kelleher, "Violence In Sports: Suspended Soccer Player Speaks Out."

29. Quoted in O'Reilly and Cahn, *Women and Sports in the United States*, p. 27

30. Quoted in O'Reilly and Cahn, *Women and Sports in the United States*, p. 28

31. Quoted in Jenée Desmond Harris, "Despite Decades of Racist and Sexist Attacks, Serena Williams Keeps Winning," *Vox*, January 28, 2017. www.vox.com.

32. Quoted in Desmond-Harris, "Despite Decades of Racist and Sexist Attacks, Serena Williams Keeps Winning."

33. Quoted in "'I'm Black So I Look Mean?' Serena Williams Discusses Race and Pregnancy," *The Guardian*, August 15, 2017. www.theguardian.com.

34. Quoted in *Playing Unfair: The Media Image of the Female Athlete*.

35. Quoted in Jaclyn Hendricks, "Empowered Aly Raisman Poses Nude for SI Swimsuit," *New York Post*, February 13, 2018. www.nypost.com.

36. Quoted in Jennifer Gish, "Nude Image of Fairfield's Julie Chu a Model For Girls," *Connecticut Post*, October 13, 2011. www.ctpost.com.

37. Quoted in "Radio Host Fired After Making Sexual Comments About Chloe Kim," *CBS News*, February 15, 2018. www.cbsnews.com.

38. Quoted in "Media Coverage of Female Athletes," *Twin Cities PBS*, December 1, 2013. www.tpt.org.

39. Quoted in Jessica Testa, "The Strongest Woman in America Lives in Poverty," *Buzzfeed News*, June 27, 2012. www.buzzfeednews.com.

40. Quoted in Kristine Solomon, "Olympic Weight Lifter Sarah Robles Shares Body-Positive Message," *Yahoo! Lifestyle*, August 16, 2016. www.yahoo.com.

41. Quoted in *Playing Unfair: The Media Image of the Female Athlete*.

42. Quoted in Associated Press, "Penn State's Portland Makes 'Difficult' Decision to Quit," *ESPN*, March 25, 2017. www.espn.com.

43. Quoted in Alex Bauer, "A Look Back at Rene Portland's 'No Lesbian' Lady Lions," *Onward State*, June 29, 2017. www.onwardstate.com.

44. Quoted in Bauer, "A Look Back at Rene Portland's 'No Lesbian' Lady Lions."

45. Quoted in Azeen Ghorayshi, "These Women Athletes Were Barred From Competing Because They Weren't 'Female' Enough," *Buzzfeed News*, August 12, 2016. www.buzzfeednews.com.

46. Quoted in Alice Park, "Woman Enough? Inside the Controversial World of Olympic Gender Testing," *Time*, July 2, 2012. www.time.com.

47. Quoted in Ariel Levy, "Either/Or: Sports, Sex, and the Case of Caster Semenya," November 30, 2009. www.newyorker.com.

48. Quoted in Jeré Longman, "Caster Semenya Will Challenge Testosterone Rule in Court," *New York Times*, June 18, 2018. www.nytimes.com.

CHAPTER 3: WHAT IS THE BUSINESS SIDE OF WOMEN AND SPORTS?

49. Quoted in Marika Washchyshyn, "Stacy Lewis Says Pay Gap Between Tours Is 'Frustrating,'" *Golf*, February 17, 2016. www.golf.com.

50. Quoted in Washchyshyn, "Stacy Lewis Says Pay Gap Between Tours Is 'Frustrating.'"

51. Quoted in Sean Zak, "2018 U.S. Women's Open Purse and Payout Breakdown," *Golf*, May 30, 2018. www.golf.com.

52. Quoted in "U.S. Women's Team Files Wage-Discrimination Action Vs. U.S. Soccer," *ESPN News*, April 1, 2016. www.espn.com.

53. Quoted in Amanda Ottaway, "Why Don't People Watch Women's Sports?" *The Nation*, July 20, 2016. www.thenation.com.

54. Quoted in Graham Hays, "Lisa Modglin Juggles Softball, Accounting," *espnW*, July 28, 2012. www.espnw.com.

55. Quoted in *Burn the Ships*. Directed by Julia Thorndike and Danielle Miller, Think Media Studios, 2017.

56. Quoted in *Burn the Ships*.

57. Quoted in O'Reilly and Cahn, *Women and Sports in the United States*, p. 311.

58. Quoted in Lisa Olson, "The #MeToo Movement Comes to Sports, a Reckoning Long Overdue," *The Athletic*, n.d. www.theathletic.com.

59. Quoted in Joanna Demkiewicz, "ESPN's New Columnist Talks Sports Writing and Underdogs," *The Riveter*, October 8, 2014. www.therivetermagazine.com.

60. Quoted in Andrew Keh, "Smashing a Ceiling and a Lot of Egos," *New York Times*, August 16, 2014. www.nytimes.com.

CHAPTER 4: WHAT IS THE FUTURE OF WOMEN AND SPORTS?

61. Quoted in Zack Pumerantz, "The 50 Most Inspirational Sports Quotes in History," *Bleacher Report*, April 23, 2012. www.bleacherreport.com.

62. Quoted in Jacob Bogage, "Youth Sports Study: Declining Participation, Rising Costs and Unqualified Coaches," *Washington Post*, September 6, 2017. www.washingtonpost.com.

63. Mary Jo Kane, "Sex Sells Sex, Not Women's Sports," *The Nation*, August 15, 2011. www.thenation.com.

64. Quoted in Andrew Good, "When It Comes to Women in Sports, TV News Tunes Out," *USC News*, June 5, 2015. news.usc.edu.

65. "Invisible Women in Sport," *Institute for Sport Social Justice*, 2018. www.sportandsocialjustice.org.

66. Quoted in Jessica Golden, "Venus and Serena Williams: Men Need to be Advocates for Pay Equality, Too," *CNBC*, March 8, 2018. www.cnbc.com.

67. Quoted in Dayna Evans, "The U.S. Women's Hockey Team Won Their Fight for Fair Pay. Here's What Needs to Happen Next," *The Cut*, March 29, 2017. www.thecut.com.

68. "The IOC, UN Women, UNESCO, P&G and NBC Are Changing the Conversation about Women in Sport," *UNESCO*, March 15, 2018. www.unesco.org.

69. "The IOC, UN Women, UNESCO, P&G and NBC Are Changing the Conversation about Women in Sport."

70. Quoted in Mary Pilon, "For Coed U.S. Open Event, Reaction Seems to Be Mixed, Too," *New York Times*, September 4, 2014. www.nytimes.com.

71. Quoted in Christopher Clarey, "Open Waters?" *New York Times*, June 21, 2018. www.nytimes.com.

72. Quoted in "This Day in History: 1926, Gertrude Ederle Becomes First Woman to Swim English Channel," *History Channel*, n.d. www.history.com.

73. Ashima Shiraishi, *Instagram*, June 11, 2018. www.instagram.com.

FOR FURTHER **RESEARCH**

BOOKS

Susan K. Cahn, *Coming on Strong: Gender and Sexuality in Women's Sport*. Urbana, IL: University of Illinois Press, 2015.

Cheryl Cooky and Michael A. Messner, *No Slam Dunk: Gender, Sport and the Unevenness of Social Change.* New Brunswick, NJ: Rutgers University Press, 2018.

L.A. Jennings, *She's a Knockout!: A History of Women in Fighting Sports*. Lanham, MD: Rowman & Littlefield, 2015.

Jennifer H. Lansbury, *A Spectacular Leap: Black Women Athletes in Twentieth-Century America*. Fayetteville, AR: University of Arkansas Press, 2014.

Molly Schiot, *Game Changers: The Unsung Heroines of Sports History.* New York: Simon and Schuster, 2016.

INTERNET SOURCES

Katie Barnes, "How Two Transgender Athletes Are Fighting to Compete in the Sports They Love," *ESPN The Magazine*, May 29, 2018. www.espn.com.

Ken Belson, "No Sweatpants in Public: Inside the Rule Books for N.F.L. Cheerleaders," *New York Times*, April 2, 2018. www.nytimes.com.

Jacob Bogage, "Youth Sports Study: Declining Participation, Rising Costs and Unqualified Coaches," *Washington Post*, September 6, 2017. www.washingtonpost.com.

Ian Crouch, "Serena Williams Is America's Greatest Athlete," *The New Yorker*, June 19, 2017. www.newyorker.com.

Linda Flanagan, "The Field Where Men Still Call the Shots," *The Atlantic*, July 28, 2017. www.theatlantic.com.

WEBSITES

espnW
www.espn.com/espnw

Part of the sports media outlet ESPN, espnW is a website that focuses exclusively on stories from the world of women in sports.

The Institute for Sport and Social Justice
www.sportandsocialjustice.org

The Institute for Sport and Social Justice aims to use the power of sports to create a more just society. It provides research and education on the intersection of sports and human rights.

Women's Sports Foundation
www.womenssportsfoundation.org

Founded by Billie Jean King, the Women's Sports Foundation conducts research, gives grants and scholarships, and speaks out on issues facing women in sports.

INDEX

ABC News, 32

Akron Racers, 48–50

All-American Girls Professional
Baseball League, 16–17, 28

Alliance of Women Coaches, 62

Amateur Sports Act of 1978, 19–20

Association for Women in Sports
Media, 62

Ayana, Almaz, 67

Baltimore Orioles, 54

Berenson, Senda, 14

Boston, Massachusetts, 51

Burn the Ships, 48

business of sports
endorsements, 16, 32, 34, 44–45
media coverage, 10, 15, 20, 22–26,
30–34, 41, 42, 48, 51–52, 60–62
pay gap, 44–49, 53, 63
sponsorships, 8–9, 34, 43–45,
50–51
women coaches and administrators,
53–55, 61–62
women in sports media, 51–53,
61–62

Chand, Dutee, 40

Chastain, Brandi, 31–32

Chicago, Illinois, 14, 59

Chicago Sun-Times, 35

Chu, Julie, 32

Cold War, 37

Cooky, Cheryl, 25, 61

Cornelius, Steve, 40–41

Davis, Bailey, 29

Detroit Tigers, 54

Duggan, Meghan, 63

Ederle, Gertrude, 68–69

English Channel, 68–69

ESPN, 25, 30, 61

ESPN The Magazine, 32, 52

espnW, 61

Excelle Sports, 61

Faut, Jean, 17

Federer, Roger, 46

Forbes, 46, 55

Fratkin, Kaleigh, 48

gender neutral sports, 64–65

gender roles, 22–24, 27, 30, 35, 37,
56, 61
femininity, 16–17, 24, 26–30, 52
masculinity, 13, 15, 24, 26, 35

gender tests, 37–40

Gerstner, Joanne, 51

Gibson, Althea, 17, 30–31

Girls in the Game, 59

Greenhalgh, Libby, 65–66

Griffin, Pat, 35–36

Guerrero, Lisa, 52

Hamlin, Erin, 60

Hamm, Mia, 21, 59

Harris, Jennifer, 36

Henie, Sonja, 16

history of women and sports
1600s to 1700s, 12–13
1800s, 13
early history, 10–12
early to mid-1900s, 13–14
mythology, 11

homophobia, 22, 35–36

Instagram, 29

Institute for Diversity and Ethics and Sports (TIDES), The, 51

Institute for Sport and Social Justice, 61

International Association of Athletics Federation (IAAF), 38–41

International Olympic Committee (IOC), 15, 37–38, 64

Invisible Women in Sport, 61–62

Joyner-Kersee, Jackie, 20–21

Kane, Mary Jo, 24, 60–61

Kempf, Cheri, 50–51

Kim, Chloe, 33–34

Kimes, Misa, 52–53

King, Billie Jean, 18–19, 58

Lambert, Elizabeth, 29–30

LaVoi, Nicole, 34

League of Their Own, A, 28

Legal Aid at Work, 58

Lewis, Stacy, 44–45

March Madness, 61

Michigan State University, 58

mixed-gender sports, 64–65

Modglin, Lisa, 50

muscle gap, 66

Musto, Michela, 24–26

Nabozny, Heather, 54

Nassar, Larry, 58

National Basketball Players Association, 55

National Football League (NFL), 26, 28–29, 51, 52, 53

National Pro Fastpitch, 48–51

National Senior Games Association, 60

National Women's Law Center, 58

National Women's Soccer League, 20

New Orleans Saints, 29

New York City, 7, 14

New York Times, 28, 69

Nike, 32, 45

Oakland Raiders, 28

Olson, Lisa, 51–52

Olympic Games, 8, 10–11, 14–15, 17, 20, 32–35, 37–38, 40–41, 46, 53, 56, 60, 64, 67–69

Paralympic Games, 20

Pearl, Bruce, 54

Pennsylvania State University, 35–36

performance gap, 66–67

Philadelphia Inquirer, 35

Play Like A Girl, 60

Portland, Rene, 35–36

Purdue University, 61

racism, 14, 17, 30–31

Raisman, Aly, 32

Riggs, Bobby, 18–19

Roberts, Michele, 55

Robles, Sarah, 34–35

Rudolph, Wilma, 17

Semenya, Caster, 38–40

sexual harassment, 51–52, 58

Sherry, Nicole, 54

Shiraishi, Ashima, 6–9, 69

Solo, Hope, 47, 59

Special Olympics, 19–20

sports
  baseball, 13–14, 16–17, 28, 48–50, 54, 60
  basketball, 13–15, 20, 35–36, 53–55, 61
  bicycling, 15
  boxing, 13
  figure skating, 16, 21, 27
  football, 13–14, 26, 28–29, 52, 53
  free diving, 67
  golf, 13–15, 44–45
  gymnastics, 20, 27, 32, 58
  hockey, 32, 48, 63
  rock climbing, 6–9, 69
  ski jumping, 64–65
  skiing, 11, 56
  soccer, 20–21, 26, 29–31, 46–47, 59
  softball, 48–51
  speed walking, 13
  tennis, 13–14, 17–19, 30–31, 44, 46, 58, 63–64
  track and field, 15, 20–21, 38–41, 64
  volleyball, 27
  weightlifting, 34, 66
  wrestling, 10–12, 18
Sports Illustrated, 15, 26, 32
SportsCenter, 24, 25
Stephens, Helen, 37–38
Stokes, Elizabeth, 13
Street, Picabo, 56
Streeter, Tanya, 67
Summitt, Pat, 53–54, 61

Tampa Bay Buccaneers, 52
Thomashaw, Amanda, 58

Title IX, 17–18, 20, 42, 48, 53, 57–58, 60
transgender athletes, 22, 40–41
Twitter, 26, 34

United Nations, 63
United States Soccer Federation, 46–47
University of Minnesota, 34
USA Hockey, 63

von Hillern, Bertha, 13

Washington, Ora, 30
Wimbledon, 17, 63
Willard, Frances, 15
Williams, Serena, 31, 46, 63
Williams, Venus, 17, 63
Women in Sports and Events, 62
Women in Sports Foundation, 45
Women's National Basketball Association (WNBA), 20, 21, 44, 53
Women's Professional Soccer, 20
Women's Sports Foundation, 58, 59
Women's United Soccer Association, 20
World War II, 16

Yearwood, Andraya, 41

Zaharias, Mildred "Babe" Didrikson, 15

IMAGE **CREDITS**

ABOUT THE **AUTHOR**

A.W. Buckey is a writer and tutor living in Brooklyn, New York.